A/B Testing

A "Hybrid" Statistical Approach

PHILIPPE AIMÉ, JOCHEN GRÜNBECK

Convertize
London, United Kingdom

© 2018 Convertize LTD.

Philippe Aimé, Jochen Grünbeck
A/B Testing: A "Hybrid" Statistical Approach

Published by: Convertize

Data Science by: Yanis Tazi

Edited by: Olivia Munk

Cover Design by: Syed Sami

A CIP record for this book is acailable from the Library of Congress Cataloging-in-Publication Data

ISBN: 9781980408291

Abstract

Marketers can easily draw incorrect conclusions from their A/B experiments if statistical analyses are not strictly followed. There are two main approaches to A/B testing: Frequentist, and Bayesian.

While Frequentist is faster, Bayesian can be more reliable. In this publication, Convertizes outlines its "hybrid" approach to A/B testing, which combines Frequentist and Bayesian analysis to provide the most reliable results as quickly as possible.

Introduction

A/B testing allows marketers to harness the power of data in order to determine which version of a particular webpage is most successful in converting browsers into buyers.

But before conducting a complete website redesign, there are several crucial statistical decisions that must be made to correctly calculate and interpret the results.

It's imperative to the success of your experiment that the data is properly applied to the appropriate statistical tests, and that the resulting information is then properly understood. If results are interpreted incorrectly, you run the risk of implementing a website variation that has not mathematically proven itself to improve sales or leads. You even run the risk of *decreasing* conversions.

Even though crunching the numbers from your testing might seem like an objective task, there are actually a number of opinions on how best to collect and analyse your results.

In A/B testing, there are two main schools of thought: Frequentist and Bayesian.

The Frequentist approach is taken when only the raw data collected from an experiment is used to make predictions. The Bayesian approach is applied when previous data and results are considered alongside the raw data of the current experiment when drawing conclusions

Say you want to see which webpage—A or B—performs best over the course of a particular Monday. At the end of that Monday, you take the data from the course of the day, calculate the statistical significance of a spike in conversions for page B, and determine that webpage B did indeed perform better than webpage A. This is the Frequentist approach.

A Bayesian approach to the same experiment would mean considering traffic and conversion data from ten previous Mondays as well the current Monday in question.

How can I choose which approach is right for me?

There are pros and cons to both approaches. The Frequentist, or "classical" approach, is faster and less complex, as it utilizes straightforward statistical calculations and a fixed data set that is only related to the specific experiment at hand. However, its limited data set increases the likelihood for the results to be merely due to chance.

The Bayesian approach is more complex, yet potentially more reliable. It relies on the assumption that if a certain outcome has been observed before, there's a greater chance that it'll happen again in the future.

For any philosophy buffs out there, Bayesian probability—coined in the 18th century by Presbyterian minister Thomas Bayes—is often believed to have been developed to counter David Hume's argument that a "miraculous" event was unlikely to be a true miracle due to the innate rarity of a miracle in the first place. Bayes potentially sought to challenge Hume by showing that future outcomes can be mathematically predicted by past occurrences, rather than an outcome's perceived rarity. As a 2014 New York Times article noted, even Hume himself might have been "impressed" when, in 2013, New York Coast Guard search and rescue teams used Bayesian statistics to successfully locate and rescue a fisherman who fell overboard in the Atlantic Ocean.

So...which one should I use?

Well, A/B testing has given us the ability to statistically analyze more data points over a shorter period of time—the Frequentist approach.

But this can potentially prevent us from getting the most accurate results possible—if we "peek" at the results and see that statistical significance has been reached, we might truncate the experiment before it is truly over due to an error. However, A/B testing also lets us introduce and accurately apply more complex statistical algorithms that take past outcomes into account—the Bayesian approach. But considering previous outcomes is more complicated and takes longer, and might be ignoring fresh data in favor of stale information.

The best approach to A/B testing is, therefore, to use the best of both in what we at Convertize call a hybrid approach.

CHAPTER ONE

Methods

What is a "hybrid approach," and how can it help my testing?

Usually, the significance level in A/B testing is computed using a fixed sample size—attributed to the frequentist approach, since reducing the sample size can produce results faster. This desire for quick results can lead to marketers calculating and checking the significance result at the end of each running day of their experiment. Many statisticians advocate a "no peeking" rule, since marketers might be tempted to end an experiment the moment statistical significance is found, but before the targeted sample size has been reached.

This "no peeking" rule is due to a statistical phenomenon called "regression to the mean." This means that if you measure an extreme data point, the next measurement will be closer to the mean. Regression to the mean can happen to your measurements because of a sampling error, such as having sample that is too small, and therefore unrepresentative of the chosen population. If you peek at the A/B results before the targeted sample size has been reached, and the results are unrepresentative of the true population due to regression to the mean, you'll be lead to incorrect conclusions.

Since conversion rates, sample sizes, and therefore all the parameters in an A/B test continually evolve over the course of the experiment, we have decided to compute the significance level every running day only after a set number of days of testing in order to give our clients robust and reliable results.

We've programmed our algorithm to wait a specific number of running days before computing the significance level because of the volatility in data gathered at the beginning of the tests, due to regression to the mean and other errors. After these initial days, we calculate and provide the significance level at the end of every running day.

Okay, I'm in—how can I use a "hybrid approach"?

To successfully use the hybrid approach, it's important to thoroughly understand the statistical tools used to calculate the results of A/B testing.

The following sections "A/B testing: the statistical basics" and "Applications in A/B testing" will go into detail regarding the basics of statistical significance, before delving into the more complicated calculations."

If you're already a seasoned pro, feel free to skip ahead! If you think you might need a refresher, read on.

CHAPTER TWO

A/B testing: the statistical basis

Statistical Significance

In A/B testing, the most important tool for interpretation is Statistical Significance—the probability that the difference between the conversion rates of two webpage variations is the result of real changes in consumer behaviour. It's a statistically robust way of proving that our results are reliable before jumping to conclusions.

Marketers and optimisation experts wait for a certain significance level before choosing the winning variation. It is the easiest way of quantifying our level of certainty that we've received significant results once we analyze the data from our A/B test.

The statistical level most widely taken to indicate that there is a 95% chance that the results are significant. This means that 19 times out of 20, the variation that we have chosen as the winning one is the true winner. The probability that the results are irrelevant and merely due to chance is 1/20. If your A/B test reveals that your results are statistically significant at a rate of $p<0.05$—probability of chance is less than 95%—then 19 times out of 20, a visitor was more likely to complete a sale on variation B rather than variation A.

Similarly, it means that 95% of the time, **our results are not due to chance.**

Sample size

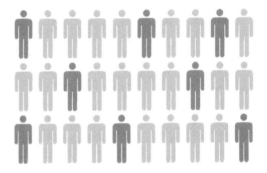

In statistics, the sample size is an important term that refers to the number of visitors used to collect data in our experiment. In the case of A/B testing, it means the number of people who have visited the two webpage variations.

In general, the larger the sample size, the more accurate the test will be.

The real danger with small datasets is that an "outlier"—or a data point that is very different in value from the rest of the results—will have a big impact on the interpreted results, and therefore the predictions.

The mean

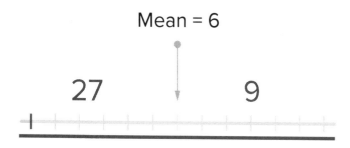

The mean simply means "the average." In A/B testing, we are measuring the mean conversion rate for each variation.

The Variance & Standard Deviation

Variance - the difference between our results and expectation

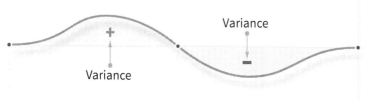

Source: http://www.thepokerbank.com/strategy/other/variance/

The Variance measures the average spread between numbers in a dataset. It measures how far each number is from the mean. Usually, we aim to minimise the variance. The smaller the variance, the better the mean is a good guess of the typical conversion rate for a particular variation.

The standard deviation expresses how the data is clustered around the mean. The smaller the standard deviation, the closer our data set is to the mean.

The Hypothesis

Before we can prove that a hypothesis—an "educated guess"—is true, or even false, we need all of the data results to support this conclusion. We therefore will need to closely examine the population of our data set. In A/B testing our hypothesis is that the "B" page we optimize with predictive notifications, calls-to-actions, customer reviews, etc. will perform better than the old page A.

Okay, got all of that? Great. It's time to start testing.

Testing our Hypothesis

In statistics, we use "hypothesis testing" to draw random samples from the population. This allows us to decide whether or not our hypothesis is true or false, and helps us avoid concluding results caused by change.

To do so, we first compare our educated guess—H1, the "alternative hypothesis"—to H0, the "null hypothesis." A null hypothesis states that there is no change in the data between the two populations in an experiment—e.g. webpages A and B in A/B testing showed the exact same conversion rates. H1 is an alternative result to H0, which represents no change in the populations despite the experimental conditions.

H0= the null hypothesis

H1= the alternative hypothesis

What we want to test is if H1 is true.

In this case, 2 outcomes are possible:

1. We reject H0 and therefore accept H1 because we have sufficient supporting evidence.

2. We cannot reject H0 because not enough evidence.

Hypothesis null

H0	True	False
Reject	Type I error	Correct decision
Accept	Correct decision	Type II error

The rejection of H0 even when H0 is true is called a Type I error. Committing this error mean that in interpreting the results, we concluded that there was a change in conversion rates between webpages A and B during testing, even though the data reveals that there was not a change.

The probability of NOT committing this error is called the "significance level" in marketers' language.

In statistics, we define H0 in order to relate it to this kind error. The Type I error is usually the error that we most want to avoid because it is more important to not commit a Type I error than it is to commit a Type II error. This is because committing a Type I error would mean seeing a change in one variation over another when there *actually was no difference* between the two variations. Thus a marketer might accidentally implement changes perceived to increase sales when there is actually no evidence for this benefit.

The acceptance of H0 when H0 is false is the Type II error. The probability of NOT committing this error is called the "power."

Relationship between type I and type II error rates

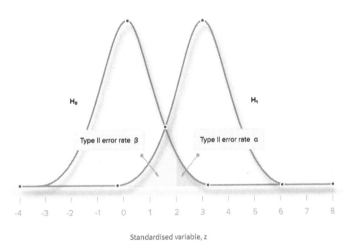

Standardised variable, z

It is important to notice that these two errors are antagonistic: we cannot try to reduce both Type I and Type II errors at the same time.

As you can see from the two bell curves, trying to decrease one of the two errors areas by moving "Any mean" will directly result in increasing the other type of error.

However, we can simultaneously reduce the probability of committing either of the two errors by increasing our sample size—in this case, the number of visitors to webpages A and B.

Reducing both Type I and Type II errors (cont.)

Original comparison of errors:

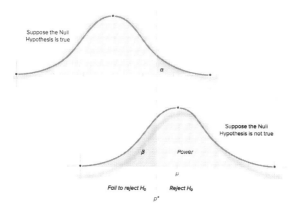

Comparison of errors with a larger sample size:

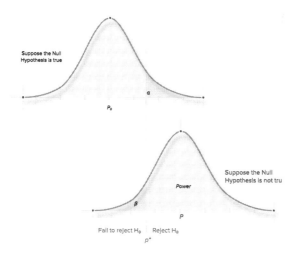

CHAPTER THREE

Applications in A/B testing

Now that you understand all the concepts and caveats behind statistical significance, it's time to apply them to our model—and to your website.

The reasoning behind A/B testing is that if we can compare two variations of the same webpage, we can use data to determine which one is the best in terms of conversion rate. Here, a "conversion" can mean a visitor registering to a page or buying a product. In our experiment, we want to find which variation of the webpage is converting more visitors into buyers or leads.

Using statistics, we can create a model that corresponds to two samples that respectively represent the number of visitors for each variation.

First, we will create two hypotheses: H0 and H1.

H0= no differences between the two groups—this means that the conversion rates of both pages are the same.

H1= there are discernible differences between the two groups—this means that the conversion rates are different.

Now, let's calculate H0 and H1 using a bit of math:

$$CRa = Ca/Na$$

This is the conversion rate for variation (webpage) A.

Here, "Ca" is the number of visitors that convert to buyers for variation A, and "Na" is the number of total visitors of variation A

$$CRb = Cb/Nb$$

This is the conversion rate for variation B.

Here, "Cb" is the number of visitors that convert for variation B, and "Nb" the number of total visitors of variation B

Thus,

H0 : CRa = CRb.   vs.   H1: CRa≠CRb

The conversion rates of variations A and B are equal for our null hypothesis, versus the conversion rates of variations A and B are not equal for our alternative hypothesis. (It is the alternative hypothesis that we seek in A/B testing so that we can determine which webpage design performs best.)

In each sample, we can only have two possibilities:

The probability that the viewer converts into a buyer:

p=CRa in variation A and p'=CRb in variation B

(Here, the variable "p" is used to denote the value of the "probability." P prime (p') is used to also stand for the value of a probability, albeit a different number and probability than p—in this case, the conversion rate of variation B.)

The probability that the viewer does not convert into a buyer:

1-p=1-CRa in variation A, and 1-p'=1-CRb in variation B.

As a statistician might point out, a **Bernoulli distribution** is at work behind this equation. A Bernoulli distribution, named after the Swiss mathematician who defined it, refers to an experiment with only two possible outcomes: 1, for "success" (or the alternative hypothesis) or 0, for "failure" (the null hypothesis). Mathematically, if p represents the probability of a successful outcome, then 1-p represents the probability of failure.

In our model, the conversion rate is represented by a **Bernoulli random variable**, meaning that it can only be represented two ways: conversion (success), or non-conversion (failure).

In statistics, there are several models that can be used to test hypotheses. The following is a commonly used model for when we want to compare two sets of data:

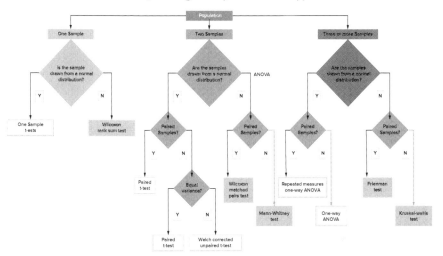

We will follow all of these steps to find which test works best for our scenario and explain the assumptions behind it.

Step 1: How many samples are there?

We have two variations. Therefore, we will draw a sample for each one, providing us with two samples.

Step 2: Normal Distribution?

To understand this, we need to understand one of the most frequently used theorems in statistics: **The Central Limit Theorem.**

The Central Limit Theorem is a statistical theory that states that given a **sufficiently large** sample size from a population with a **finite variance** (meaning a distribution book-ended by 2 discrete values), the sample proportion will result in an approximately **normal distribution** (a commonly used distribution of data that states that the majority of a population will fall around the average).

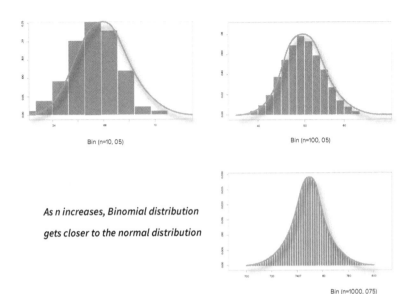

Bin (n=10, 05)

Bin (n=100, 05)

As n increases, Binomial distribution gets closer to the normal distribution

Bin (n=1000, 075)

A Binomial distribution is a distribution that can have two results. A Bernoulli distribution is a kind of binomial distribution, where there are two results for an experiment that has been carried out for just one trial (n=1).As we can see, the shape of the Binomial (including Bernoulli) distribution tends to follow the shape of a typical bell curve (a normal distribution). The Binomial distribution is essentially the result of many, many Bernoulli distributions being averaged together so that we can find which result, p or 1-p, conversion or non-conversion, occurs most often. Thus, the larger our sample size, the more accurate our results.

In A/B testing, the number of visitors to a site is typically large enough to be considered as an adequately substantial sample size.

Step 3: Paired or unpaired samples?

In A/B testing, we're dealing with **unpaired samples**. Data is described as unpaired when the sets of data arise from separate individuals.

Step 4: Variance?

Since the variance between the two variations have no reason to be equal, we're dealing with **unequal variances.**

Conclusion:

Using the decision-tree above to find the test, the **Welch corrected unpaired** test is the appropriate statistical tool.

The most important thing to do is to understand the data that we have collected (how many samples and if they are paired or unpaired) and the statistical terms and concepts. This will lead us to the correct decision.

Now that we have all this, we can finally compute the significance level of our data.

Welch's t-test:

In statistics, **Welch's t-test**, or an unequal variances t-test, is a two-sample location test used to test the hypothesis that two populations have equal means when the variances and the sample sizes are unequal. It is an adaptation of **Student's t-test** (a test that both compares two means and tells you how different they are from each other, and can determine whether this difference is significant) for unpaired t-tests. If variances are equal, the two t-tests lead to the same results.

We need to decide which approach are we going to use. There are two to choose from: **a one-tailed test** versus a **two-tailed test**. Since we do not have any prior indication as to which variation is better, and we only want to determine if the two means are different, we'll need to use a two-tailed approach. A common mistake is to use a one tailed approach, because it only allows us to determine if a mean is greater than the other. This incorrectly forces us to choose a direction prior to testing, corrupting the results.

One-tailed approach

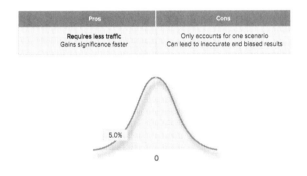

Pros	Cons
Requires less traffic Gains significance faster	Only accounts for one scenario Can lead to inaccurate and biased results

Two-tailed approach

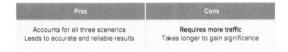

Pros	Cons
Accounts for all three scenerios Leads to accurate and reliable results	**Requires more traffic** Takes longer to gain significance

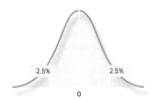

In Welch's t-test, we need to compute two parameters in order to find the statistical significance.

First, we calculate the t value:

$$t = \frac{CRa - CRb}{\sqrt{\dfrac{Sa^2}{Na} + \dfrac{Sb^2}{Nb}}}$$

where Sa and Sb are the Empirical Standard Deviation (the amount of variation within a data set) of variation A and variation B.

$$Sa = \sqrt{\frac{1}{Na-1}\left[Ca \cdot (1 - CRa)^2 + (Na - Ca) \cdot CRa^2 \right]}$$

$$Sb = \sqrt{\frac{1}{Nb-1}\left[Cb \cdot (1 - CRb)^2 + (Nb - Cb) \cdot CRb^2 \right]}$$

The second one is the **degree of freedom**:

$$k = \frac{\left(\dfrac{Sa^2}{Na} + \dfrac{Sb^2}{Nb} \right)^2}{\dfrac{Sa^4}{Na^2 \cdot (Na - 1)} + \dfrac{Sb^4}{Nb^2 \cdot (Nb - 1)}}$$

A degree of freedom (represented here as k) is an approximation of the independent pieces of information that were incorporated into the statistical analysis. This is different from the sample size in that the degree of freedom is the sample size -1, or n-1. This is the amount of data points that are "free to vary," or the amount of data points that can differ in value from the mean without changing the value of the mean.

Then, we can use the values of t and k in the t-distribution to test the null hypothesis and find the significance level.

As you can see, understanding the concept of significance level in A/B testing is pretty complicated, and this is why marketers might not understand their results—or even worse, conclude the incorrect results.

Conclusion

How Convertize uses the hybrid approach

Convertize's hybrid approach will provide you with the most accurate results possible over the shortest possible amount of time.

If we were to calculate the data from A/B testing exactly as described above, we would be calculating it using the **Frequentist** method.

However, when combined with the following **weighting** according to **how results change over the course of the experiment** and taking into account **the difference in consumer behaviour on different days of the week**, we add the **Bayesian** approach to our calculations.

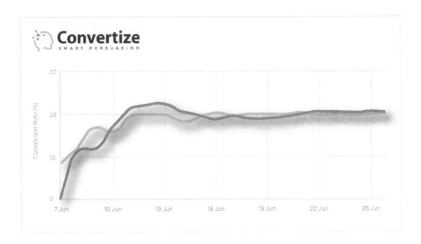

For an example of what this hybrid approach might look like for your own A/B testing, look at the above results of an experiment from our own website.

At the beginning of the experiment, you can see that it might be easy to conclude incorrect results. Initially, the grey variation is markedly more successful than the red variation; yet over time, it is the red variation that proves to be the more successful variation.

One of the most common errors in A/B testing is calculating the significance level—which tells us the confidence level, or risk tolerance, of a particular variation—to directly draw conclusions. The significance calculation makes a critical assumption that most marketers violate without even realizing: that the sample size is fixed.

In fact, the significance level changes with the sample size.

Intuitively, the higher the confidence level in the results, the higher the sample size should be. This is true, but not enough to generate statistical significance.

In fact, as the sample sizes change, the conversion rates of the two variations also changes, and this affects the significance level. The problem with this is also visible in the graphic above. This statistical phenomenon means that when many variables are at play, an extreme data point tends to be preceded or followed by one that is closer to the mean.

Therefore, the smaller is the difference between the two conversion rates, the lower our significance level. This is why it's hard to systematically draw conclusions—those two terms, like trying to both minimize the probability of committing a Type I and a Type II error, can be antagonistic.

Our smart algorithms are aware of these phenomena when they compute the significance level over the course of A/B testing. They update the sample sizes and the conversion rates, providing you with accurate and reliable results. The goal is to make sure you collect enough data points to confidently make predictions or changes based on the results.

Be aware of the days of the week

Another issue with collecting data in A/B testing is ensuring you are highly cognizant as to which days of the week you're collecting your data on. User behaviour will be different on a weekend as compared to a weekday. In our hybrid approach, it's important to weight days with different kinds of user behaviour differently.

To solve this problem, we're going to introduce a new way to calculate the mean of the two variations each day in order to incorporate the changing data over time.

The conversion rate for users who visit on a Tuesday is not going to be the same for users who visit on a Saturday. This needs to be taken into account when carrying out A/B testing, yet online marketers often ignore this issue when optimizing websites.

Since we are going to compute the significance level every running day, we will give different weights to the previous daily conversion rates in order to calculate an average conversion rate that is the most significant.

In simpler terms, if we give the same weight to the daily conversion rate, the first day that we begin the experiment will have the same impact on the significance level as the last running days, which is incorrect and can corrupt our results. A lot of events happen over time and the closer the experiment is to the last running day, the more the impact of the data is important.

To resolve this, we will create a new function to calculate CRa and CRb over time.

CRa will now be a weighted average of the conversion rates of all the days until this running day for variation A.

Similarly, CRb will be a weighted average of the conversion rates of all the days until this running day for variation B:

$$weightedAverageCRb = \sum_{i=1}^{lastRunningDay} \left(\frac{i}{\sum_{j=1}^{lastRunningDay} j} \right) * CRb(i)$$

$$weightedAverageCRa = \sum_{i=1}^{lastRunningDay} \left(\frac{i}{\displaystyle\sum_{j=1}^{lastRunningDay} j} \right) * CRa(i)$$

Thus:

CRa(i) is the conversion rate of variation A for the day i

CRb(i) is the conversion rate of variation B for the day i

When we calculate an accurate significance level every running day, we need to put more weight on the conversion rate of the closest day to this day.

This is why we have introduced this weighted function as an increasing function of the days that have passed.

When properly weighted,

$$\sum_{i=1}^{lastRunningDay} \left(\frac{i}{\displaystyle\sum_{j=1}^{lastRunningDay}} \right) = 1$$

The changing values, according to proper weighting, changes the values of t and k in the Welch test. This will give us a more realistic view of the significance level than if we took the daily results at face value.

Carrying out A/B testing properly isn't easy—but we can make it work for your website.

As you can see, it's incredibly important to understand the statistics behind A/B testing in order to be able to produce significant changes that will not corrupt the complicated theorems behind these concepts. Understanding the mathematical aspects of your A/B testing will allow you to make improvements to the algorithms by changing certain formulas to make them more realistic, and therefore allowing you to obtain more accurate results.

Now that you really understand how A/B testing works, why not give it a shot? The Convertize platform will help you set up and run experiments on your website, with no coding or statistical analyses required on your part. Let us do the heavy lifting and complicated calculations. Try it free today.

Discover the "hybrid approach" behind our Autopilot Mode™

Autopilot Mode is a powerful new feature that automatically pushes visitors to the best-converting variant.

With Autopilot engaged, you can leave Convertize in the pilot's seat of your experiments, ensuring reliable results AND maximum conversions!

Register on **convertize.com** and try it now for free.

Printed in Poland
by Amazon Fulfillment
Poland Sp. z o.o., Wrocław

59274724R00019